Wherever You Need Me

The Anna Urda Busby Story

Wherever You Need Me

The Anna Urda Busby Story

By Anna Urda Busby

Arizona Memorial Museum Association
Hawaii Guam Saipan

This work was originally published by The Tennessee Valley Press, Inc.
First printing, November 2001. Second printing, November 2002.

Photos from author's collection unless otherwise noted.
Printed in Hawaii, USA.

ISBN 0-9778183-3-0

Contents

INTRODUCTION

Welcome to the first in a new series of monographs produced by the Arizona Memorial Museum Association. In this "Personal History" series, AMMA will try to focus on a particular person whose story reflects an eyewitness account of history. Along with the personal account, we hope to provide a certain amount of context that will allow the reader a general sense of where the person was, what their job was, and who they worked with.

Anna Urda Busby's story, as well as her collected White Cap Sketches, are important not only as additions to the vast Pearl Harbor historical data that already exists, but as a look at stories not often heard. On December 7, 1941 nurses across the island of Oahu performed miracles of compassion, caring, and medical service saving hundreds of lives. Their dedication helped the U.S. overcome the devastation and despondency of defeat and rise from the ashes of Pearl Harbor.

We'd like to thank Anna Busby for letting AMMA publish her story.

DEDICATION

It has been almost 60 years since America was attacked by the Japanese at Pearl Harbor, Hawaii on December 7, 1941. Many people have forgotten about what happened on the day of infamy. This part of United States history has been told in print and video, but very few were actual Pearl Harbor survivors. The author of this book experienced it first-hand.

This lady was an Army nurse at a hospital in Honolulu, Hawaii on that fateful Sunday morning when the attack began at 7:55 a.m.

She has been making people aware of that event by writing poems and stories of the day since the late 1950s. She has worked to help organize the Alabama Pearl Harbor Survivors Association (PHSA) in 1969 and served as its co-chairperson.

From 1969 until the present, every PHSA president has requested that she continue to serve as the National Chairperson, White Caps. White Caps include the Army and Navy Nurse Corps nurses who were in military service in Hawaii on December 7, 1941.

This book will help keep the motto, "Remember Pearl Harbor, Keep America Alert" before the public.

Thanks to that nurse, Anna Urda Busby.

Norman O. Parker
Past Alabama Chairman
Pearl Harbor Survivors Association

Acknowledgements

Although manuscripts often have to undergo revisions from recordings to disks, typing, editorial ideas, additions and deletions, the author expresses appreciation to the many people who helped her with this project: Press and Author Club members, Alabama Poetry Society and Creative Writers of Montgomery.

Many thanks also go to Anna Brown and the staff at Barnes and Noble in Montgomery.

Special thanks to Helen Blackshear, who helped with recordings and editing.

I'm grateful to Colonel Robert S. Bartmettler and Anna Carmichael.

Finally, this book was made possible because of help from my husband, Sherrill, and Bruce W. Sanborn, both of whom inspired me to get things done.

This book has been a joyful project and challenge from 1946-2007.

Anna Urda Busby

A History of the Army Nurse Corps

"The Army nurse is the symbol to the soldier of help and relief in his hour of direst need. Through mud and mire, through the mark of campaign and battle, wherever the fight leads, she patiently – gallantly – seeks the wounded and distressed. Her comfort knows no parallel. In the heart of all fighting men, she is enshrined forever."

General Douglas MacArthur, Dec 44

February 2, 2005, marks the 104th anniversary of the establishment of the Army Nurse Corps. Since 1901, Army nurses have demonstrated again and again their total commitment to the highest standards of military nursing excellence. Both men and women have served as Army nurses since 1775, but the Army Nurse Corps did not become a part of the Army Medical Department until 1901. The distinguished contributions of female contract nurses during and following the 1898 Spanish-American War became the justification and demonstrated the need for a permanent female nurse corps.

More than 59,000 American nurses served in the Army Nurse Corps during World War II. Nurses worked closer to the front lines than they ever had before. Within the "chain of evacuation" established by the Army Medical Department during the war, nurses served under fire in field hospitals and evacuation hospitals, on hospital trains and hospital ships, and as flight nurses on medical transport planes. The skill and dedication of these nurses contributed to the extremely low post-injury mortality rate among American military forces in every theater of the war. Overall, fewer than 4 percent of the American soldiers who received medical care in the field or underwent evacuation died from wounds or disease.

In Europe, Army nurses assisted in developing the concept of recovery wards for immediate postoperative nursing care. Military nursing gained a greater understanding of the process of shock, blood replacement, and resuscitation. Air evacuation from the combat zone by fixed wing aircraft brought patients to definitive treatment quickly. Army flight nurses helped to establish the incredible record of only five deaths in flight per 100,000 patients.

Nurses endured hardships caring for their patients. In May 1942, with the fall of Corregidor in the Philippines, 67 Army nurses became Japanese prisoners of war. During the thirty-seven month captivity, the women endured primitive conditions and starvation rations, yet they continued to care for the ill and injured in the internment hospital. On Anzio, nurses dug their foxholes outside their tents and cared for patients under German shellfire. Their example bolstered the spirits of the soldiers who shared the same tough experience.

Recent years have seen Army nurses active throughout the world both in armed conflicts and humanitarian endeavors. In 1983, they supported combat troops in Grenada; in 1989 in Panama; and in 1991 in the Middle East. Since December 1995, Army nurses have been deployed with medical units in support of NATO alliance troops in Haiti, Bosnia, Herzegovina and Kosovo. Nurses have continued to serve proudly during relief efforts following natural disasters such as Hurricane Mitch in 1998. Today, the legacy of these military nurses lives on. Currently, Army nurses serve throughout the world in support of multiple military and humanitarian actions in support of the Global War On Terrorism.

The Army Nurse Corps listed fewer than 1,000 nurses on its rolls on 7 December 1941, the day of the Japanese surprise attack on Pearl Harbor. Eighty-two Army nurses were stationed in Hawaii serving at three Army medical facilities that infamous morning. Tripler Army Hospital was overwhelmed with hundreds of casualties suffering from severe burns and shock. The blood-spattered entrance stairs led to hallways where wounded men lay on the floor awaiting surgery. Nurses at Schofield Hospital and Hickam Field faced similar difficult circumstances. Army and Navy nurses and medics (enlisted men trained as orderlies) worked side by side with civilian nurses and doctors. As a steady stream of seriously wounded servicemen continued to arrive through the early afternoon, appalling shortages of medical supplies became apparent. Army doctrine kept medical supplies under lock and key, and bureaucratic delays prevented the immediate replacement of quickly used up stocks. Working under tremendous pressure, medical personnel faced shortages of instruments, suture material, and sterile supplies. Doctors performing major surgery passed scissors back and forth from one table to another. Doctors and nurses used cleaning rags as face masks and operated without gloves.

Six months after the Japanese bombed Pearl Harbor, there were 12,000 nurses on duty in the Army Nurse Corps. Few of them had previous military experience, and the majority reported for duty ignorant of Army methods and protocol. Only in July 1943 did Lt. Gen. Brehon B. Somervell, Commanding General, Army Service Forces, authorize a formal four-week training course for all newly commissioned Army nurses. This program stressed Army organization; military customs and courtesies; field sanitation; defense against air, chemical, and mechanized attack; personnel administration; military requisitions and correspondence, and property responsibility. From July 1943 through September 1945 approximately 27,330 newly inducted nurses graduated from fifteen Army training centers.

Nurse anesthetists were in short supply in every theater of operations, so the Army developed a special training program for nurses interested in that specialty. More than 2,000 nurses trained in a six-month course designed to teach them how to administer inhalation anesthesia, blood and blood derivatives, and oxygen therapy as well as how to recognize, prevent, and treat shock.

Nurses specializing in the care of psychiatric patients were also in great demand. One out of every twelve patients in Army hospitals was admitted for psychiatric care, and the Army discharged approximately 400,000 soldiers for psychiatric reasons. The Surgeon General developed a twelve-week program to train nurses in the care and medication of these patients.

Public health administrators as well as the American public believed that the increasing demands of the U.S. armed forces for nurses were responsible for a shortage of civilian nurses. Responding to these concerns in June 1943, Congress passed the Bolton Act, which set up the Cadet Nurse Corps program. The U.S. government subsidized the education of nursing students who promised that following graduation they would engage in essential military or civilian nursing for the duration of the war. The government also subsidized nursing schools willing to accelerate their program of study and provide student nurses with their primary training within two and a half years. Cadet nurses spent the last six months of their training assigned to civilian or military hospitals, which helped to alleviate the critical nursing shortage. Possible assignments included hospitals run by the Army, Navy, Veterans Administration, Public Health Service, and Bureau of Indian Affairs. The Cadet Nurse Corps training program was extremely successful and enjoyed enthusiastic public support. By 1948 when the program was discontinued, more than 150,000 nurse graduates testified to its value.

In December 1943 the U.S. War Department decided that there were enough nurses in the Army Nurse Corps to meet both existing and anticipated future demands on the Army. Consequently, the Army instructed the American Red Cross, which throughout the war had been responsible for the recruitment of nurses for the Army Nurse Corps, to stop recruiting. The Red Cross sent telegrams to local volunteer committees in every state advising them to discontinue their sustained drive to enlist nurses.

During the spring of 1944 intensive planning for the Allied invasion of France and the high number of anticipated casualties gave the Army second thoughts. Late in April the War Department advised the War Manpower Commission that it was revising its earlier decision to stop recruiting nurses. A new quota for the Army Nurse Corps was set at 50,000 10,000 more than were then enrolled. The Surgeon General promptly announced that the Army Nurse Corps was 10,000 nurses short, leading some critics to charge that American nurses were shirking their duty and avoiding military service. Yet nurses who responded to the much publicized "shortfall" and tried to enlist were hindered by the collapse of the local Red Cross recruiting networks.

In his January 1945 State of the Union Address President Franklin D. Roosevelt remarked that there was a critical shortage of Army nurses and that medical units in the European theater were being strained to the breaking point. He proposed that nurses be drafted. A nurse draft bill passed in the House and came within one vote in the Senate before the surrender of Germany. In the interim, thc cnrollmcnt of over 10,000 nurses in the Army Nurse Corps early in 1945 rendered the measure superfluous.

Army nurses served throughout the Pacific in increasing numbers between 7 December 1941 and the end of the war. The Army nurse in the Pacific theater performed her tasks efficiently, compassionately, and courageously whether she was caring for casualties in the field or patients evacuated from the front lines. These nurses prevailed over dangers and difficulties not experienced by nurses in other theaters. They became ill with malaria and dengue fever; experienced the rigors of a tropical climate; tolerated water shortages; risked kamikaze attacks; adapted to curfews, fenced compounds, and armed escorts; and dealt with medical corpsmen's hostility. Nurses in the Pacific demonstrated their ability to overcome adversity and reached the front lines of a uniquely dangerous theater before the end of the war.

World War II ended with the surrender of Japan in September 1945, and Army nurses stationed around the world began planning to return home. They could look back on their service with great pride. Their accomplishments were many. Nurses had been a part of every link in the chain of evacuation established in every theater of the war. Their work contributed significantly to the low mortality rate experienced by American casualties of all types.

Nurses received 1,619 medals, citations, and commendations during the war, reflecting the courage and dedication of all who served. Sixteen medals were awarded posthumously to nurses who died as a result of enemy fire. Overall, 201 nurses died while serving in the Army during the war.

Army nurses returning to civilian life discovered a changed postwar society. The tremendous manpower needs faced by the United States during World War II created numerous new social and economic opportunities for American women. Both society as a whole and the United States military found an increasing number of roles for women. The place of women in American society had been irrevocably altered and expanded by the entrance of women into professional and industrial jobs previously reserved for men. Most important for nurses, however, was society's enhanced perception of nursing as a valued profession. The Army reflected this changing attitude in June 1944 when it granted its nurses officers' commissions and full retirement privileges, dependents' allowances, and equal pay. Moreover, the government provided free education to nursing students between 1943 and 1948.

Veteran nurses also brought home with them valuable skills and experiences, increasing their professional status and self-esteem. The Army had trained significant numbers of nurses in specialties such as anesthesia and psychiatric care, and nurses who had served overseas had acquired practical experience otherwise unobtainable. Those assigned to field and evacuation hospitals had become accustomed to taking the initiative, making quick decisions, and adopting innovative solutions to a broad range of medical-related problems. They had learned organizational skills by moving and setting up field and evacuation hospitals while following the troops and had developed teaching and supervisory skills while training the corpsmen under their command. Paperwork no longer intimidated them, as circumstances had forced them to deal with increasingly complex administrative chores.

Military service took men and women from small towns and large cities across America and transported them around the world. Their wartime experiences broadened their lives as well as their expectations. After the war, many veterans, including nurses, took advantage of the increased educational opportunities provided for them by the government.

Throughout its history, the Army Nurse Corps has earned the deep respect and gratitude of the American people because of its dedication to providing the best possible care to our soldiers and their families while serving our country in war and peace. Army nurses have unselfishly come to the aid of victims of disaster and disease throughout the world. Over time, the mission has grown broader, yet there has been one constant – the devotion of the individual nurse in providing excellent nursing care.

Today, as our soldiers stand on point for our nation, defending freedom across the globe, they can rest assured, should they get wounded or ill, an Army nurse will be by their side during their hour of need. Because any time our nation calls: READY, CARING, AND PROUD, Army nurses always respond.

Source: Army Nurse Corps Historical Collection documents summarized by MAJ Debora Cox, Past ANC Historian (1 August 2001).

This brochure was prepared in the U.S. Army Center of Military History by Judith A. Bellafaire.

Chapter One

The Early Years

Our family emigrated from Galicia, Austria via Hamburg, Germany in 1893, settling in the small Pennsylvania township of Jermyn, located at the foothills of the Poconos. My mother, Kathryn, raised seven children. Bill, John, Michael, and Peter were older than I, with Joseph and Stephen following 10 and 12 years after my birth.

The family was self-sufficient, relying on farming and coal mining to help make ends meet. Every year, mother planted a vegetable garden and fruit trees, and the family tended to a small collection of farm animals that included a cow, hens, pigs, rabbits and dogs. In the winter, the cellar shelves were filled with canned fruits and vegetables for as long as mother lived at this address.

Winter in Jermyn meant snow, bobsleds and skating. When there was enough snow, the children would build snowmen in the garden, using small bits of coal to create the eyes, nose, brows and mouth. Sometimes there would be enough snow for us to make igloos that were big enough to fit two or three small children. We loved the bobsled that grandfather made for us. Michael, who was called Curly because of his hair, would steer down the hill on Hudson Street across from the cemetery. The hill consisted of three blocks with no cars, so we were safe. Over the years, we memorized every bump and curve. Life in Jermyn was simple then. The strains and stresses of today's world were not as visible. Women in the community spent their spare time quilting, sewing and crocheting. There were plenty of bazaars and social basket affairs to attend, and square dances often were held at the fire station hall.

My first experience with death came when I was 10 years old. My grandfather died suddenly at home in his bed after suffering a cerebral hemorrhage on October 4, 1922. He was very tall, handsome and elegant. A neighbor delivered the news of my grandfather's death at an early hour. I remember my mother wallpapering the front parlor of the house before my grandfather was placed in the casket. My mother and grandmother folded his clothes and gave them to the needy. My grandfather's passing was calm. Death was not feared in our family. Tears were shed softly and privately.

My father died when I was 14. It was the Sunday morning before Easter on April 26, 1926. He loved farming, but it was working in the coal mines that contributed to his death. He had been ill on several occasions with what doctors diagnosed as pneumonia. A private nurse stayed with him for several days. When he finally recovered, I decided that one day I would become a registered nurse. It was something I never forgot.

In our family, the dying were never unattended. It's difficult to put into words the rewarding feeling one receives when care is given to someone you love.

Two years after my father died, my mother remarried and moved to Jersey City with my two youngest brothers. My four older brothers and I stayed behind in Jermyn. Mother wanted me to go with her, but when I heard her husband-to-be say that I could find a job and finish high school by attending night school, the idea did not appeal to me at all.

Occasionally, I worked at Crystal Lake Country Club ironing table napkins or running errands for an elderly couple that lived across from the high school. I also helped serve dinners for small parties at the home of Dr. and Mrs. Baker. One day, Mrs. Baker gave me some advice that I never forgot.

"When you become a nurse and marry, always take a few days vacation from your husband," she said.

I graduated from Jermyn High School on June 10, 1930. Over the next two years, all four of my older brothers married girls from the

Left picture: Baby Anna middle front row with brothers Peter and Michael on either side of her, brothers Bill and John top row. Right: Peter, John and Baby Anna. Both pictures taken in 1912.

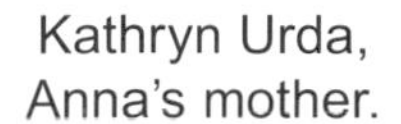

Kathryn Urda, Anna's mother.

Right: Eight year-old Anna in1920.

neighborhood. All of my girlfriends were marrying in their teens. But me? My one desire was to pursue a career in nursing. The greatest day of my life came in 1934, when I entered Hackensack Hospital's School of Nursing.

Hackensack Hospital was opened in 1888, and two years later, the School of Nursing was established. When I enrolled in the three-year program, it was under the directorship of Marie Wooders, a wonderful person who had great influence upon her students.

I loved every moment of the time I spent at nursing school. Many of my classmates were from nearby. I recall some that came from as far away as New Orleans, Puerto Rico and even some European countries. Miss Wooders always offered support to her students. "You are the best students, the best class I've ever had," she would say. I believed her at the time but still wondered if there would ever be enough time to read all of the medical books that had been written. There were so many mysteries to life and human behavior. There were some unforgettable experiences during my time at the School of Nursing between 1934-37, including my first baby delivery.

It may be hard to believe, but it was at nursing school where I first learned about sex, gonorrhea and syphilis. One 15-year-old girl, who was about to deliver her first baby, didn't even know how she became pregnant. Miss Wooders would often remind her students about their future. "Don't think you know it all when you finish at this school," she would say. "As long as you practice nursing, you must continue to learn and keep up with the trends." This was the forerunner to the continuing education program that was established in the 1960s.

Today, we don't say that nurses are trained. Instead, we say that they have been educated. Miss Wooders taught us about more than just nursing. A common question on her exams was, "Who is the most important person in the hospital?" The answer was always the same: the patient. "That is why you are here," she would remind us. It was a lesson I never forgot.

During our senior year, Miss Wooders arranged for us to visit a Buddhist temple in New York City, a Chinese temple and Mohammedan services and Presbyterian services. "Try to learn something about all religions and respect the patient's right to believe as he wishes," Miss

Wooders said. From then on, I visited various churches each Sunday and it felt wonderful to do so.

Those weren't the only trips we took. Miss Wooders also arranged for us to visit centers for lodging where meals were served to thousands of homeless men. I will never forget my first and only trip to the New York Bowery mission where men sat up day and night to keep out of the cold.

In those days, students were not allowed to marry. I had to make a choice between marriage and nursing. I chose nursing. Nursing schools in those days were considered enlightened. Interpersonal relationships and the emotional needs of students were not considered. We were student nurses that belonged to a prideful group with common aims and common sacrifices.

My schedule was hectic. Daytime sleep had to be juggled around my class schedule. It was horrible to get up during the middle of the day around 1 p.m., go to class and then come home and try to go back to sleep again. In those years, who could not muster a Florence Nightingale-type dedication? Character and a dedicated personality had to be present from the start. Training meant just that: learning and practicing skills. The emphasis was placed on learning and procedures. It wasn't until the 1960s that the nursing profession became preoccupied with its professional status. Nurses were taught by nursing specialists. No longer did nurses stand up when a doctor entered a nursing station.

In today's medical world, technology demands far more of nursing. When I entered the real world of nursing as a graduate registered nurse, I was full of enthusiasm and idealism, and ready to set the world on fire. I loved every service - medical, surgical, pediatric and obstetrics - and enjoyed an affiliation at the Soho Hospital for contagious diseases and mental nursing at Graystone Park Hospital in New Jersey.

There were many tempting nursing positions available, but the stardust of my student days had not worn off. When asked what my nursing preferences were, I simply replied that I wanted to be a bedside nurse and give excellent care. And soon I became a bedside nurse, frustrated at having to care for six patients instead of just one or two. My duties included taking blood pressures, temperature and pulse rates, giving medications and baths. In the 1930s, there were very few medications that were administered. In addition to caring for my six patients, I found out that I was responsible for six more patients for three hours each day while their nurse went off duty. Sometimes, I felt as though I were playing leapfrog, jumping from patient to patient.

After only a few weeks as a staff nurse, I was promoted to a float nurse. That meant that I worked wherever I was needed in the hospital. It also meant that I could initiate some of my own ideas for improving the practice in the hospital. My other duties included handling charts, posting lab slips, adding progress sheets to charts and writing reports. Today, secretaries handle most of those duties and it never occurred to me then that those would no longer be considered nursing duties after the 1960s.

Even though I was a float nurse, the obstetrical unit was my favorite place in the hospital – especially when everything went well and I could hold a newborn baby.

I lived in the graduate nurse's quarters next to the hospital. My salary was $70 per month and included room, board, laundry and medical care. But times were tough, and the Depression was taking a toll on everyone. At that time, we just felt lucky to have a roof over our heads. The medical care came in handy twice as I battled through pneumonia and an emergency appendectomy. My favorite doctors were Dr. John Decker, Dr. Webb and Dr. Walowitz. Each one helped me through my sickness.

There were good times, too. One night on the pediatrics ward, two boys around 5 or 6 years old were admitted for appendectomies. There were no recovery rooms back then. Patients were returned from the operating room to the ward, and a nurse remained with the patient checking vital signs until they fully recovered from the anesthesia. This particular night, one of the little boys told me to take care of the other one first. A couple of nights later, I was attending to one of the boys. After I held his hand for a moment, he said, "When I grow up, I'm going to marry you." It was my first proposal.

In 1939, after two years at Hackensack Hospital, I turned in my notice of resignation so that I could join the Army Nurse Corps. But first, I had to join the American Red Cross – a requirement before you could become a member of the Army Nurse Corps. Six months later, an opening became available and I was issued the letter N, which stood for nurse, and the number 703180. I was commissioned as a Second Lieutenant. My first

Anna with her choir friends in 1922. Anna is in the second row with the long curls.

Hackensack Hospital and School of Nursing in 1934.

assignment was at Fort Jay, Governor's Island, N.Y. I received my basic training there and learned even more from my roommate, Sally Entrekin. She informed me about the differences in rank and told me that nurses associated with officers and not enlisted men. I also got a quick lesson in protocol. One day, I had an appointment at the beauty shop on Fort Jay. Although I arrived early for my appointment, an officer's wife was taken ahead of me even though she had just phoned for an appointment.

I loved parties and dancing and one night the nurses held a party at the officers' quarters. The laughter and music disturbed a General, who asked the military police to tell us to quiet down.

The first Christmas party whetted my appetite for Hawaii. Some of the older nurses who had seen service in Hawaii and the Philippines returned with beautiful trunks, Oriental rugs, china and hula skirts. When asked by the chief nurse which foreign assignment I would like, I picked Newport, Rhode Island, so Hawaii would be my next stop.

In May and September 1940, I was assigned transport duty in the Panama Canal Zone. The first visit was aboard the USS *Chateau Thierry*. Our ship was transporting officers, troops and families. I don't recall many of my duties, but I do remember having fun playing bridge and enjoying the sea breezes. My second trip to the Canal Zone was aboard the USS *Hunter Liggett*, but only officers and troops were aboard. I was one of only two women aboard and passed many hours in the day playing bridge.

I was transferred to Fort Adams in Newport, Rhode Island, in November 1940. The base was located on Narragansett Bay. Newport was America's first resort, a colonial city with much charm, glamour and wealth. Many of the wealthiest families built mansions for summer residences in Newport, and in the winter they would leave for Palm Beach, Florida. Newport's most famous mansion, the Breakers, is now a museum with a 10-mile cliff walk. Also, the ocean drive had an unrivaled view of the Atlantic Ocean and shore.

Dating in Newport consisted of yachting, bowling, dancing, ping-pong and bridge with many of the officers. As Christmas neared, a young lieutenant named Bill Lappin asked what I would like for a gift. "A trip to Hawaii," I answered.

"I cannot give you a trip to Hawaii. I'm only a second lieutenant," he said.

Lappin offered me a three-carat diamond ring for Christmas, but I didn't accept it. Instead, he gave me a rosary and a gold compact engraved with my initials. Once again, I chose Hawaii instead of marriage. Six months later, I was assigned to Tripler General Hospital in Hawaii.

In June, 1941, all I could think of was my impending trip to Hawaii. Upon leaving Fort Adams, I was allowed 30 days leave, and went home to stay with my mother and two brothers in upstate New York.

When it was time to leave my brothers, Steve and Joseph, who were in high school, went with me to Penn Station in New York City. Several other friends came along as well. After some initial confusion with my ticket, I was assigned a parlor car for the three-day cross-country trip to San Francisco. There were some quick hugs and goodbyes by everyone, and finally I was on the train headed to Fort Mason. Fort Mason was the debarkation point for Hawaii. I spent a week there, dating officers and touring San Francisco. It was my first time to experience anything like that. It was most beautiful.

While waiting for passage to Hawaii, I heard rumors about Colonel Charles Lindbergh. It was a time when socialism and communism were thought of as bad words, and he was regarded as a fanatic. He had many political enemies during World War II. His father did not live to see Stalin, Hitler and Mussolini transform Europe into an armed camp. And it was sad that his father did not see his son fly the Atlantic and become a hero and an idol. Many years later, Col. Charles Lindbergh was commemorated with a statue that was placed in the Twin Cities of Minnesota. Known as "The Lone Eagle," Lindbergh was praised by kings, diplomats and warlords. Later, he worked at the Rockefeller Institute of Research long before I did in 1957. Learning about research in medicine was one of the highlights of my life.

After a week at Fort Mason, we finally sailed for Hawaii aboard the Mariposa. The Lurline and Mariposa were considered sister ships. They were great ocean liners, and luminaries such as Mary Pickford would sail on them for extended stays in the Hawaiian Islands. It was very glamorous.

In all, there must have been about 20 or 30 nurses on the Mariposa. Some were assigned to Schofield Hospital, which was a short distance from Tripler. When we arrived in Honolulu about 7 in the morning, the first thing we saw was Diamond Head. Hawaiian music was playing and it was

was lovely. We were greeted by several nurses, who each gave us a flower lei when we docked. One of the nurses who greeted us was Madelyn Blonsky, who was perhaps the most beautiful nurse I've ever seen. She and I became good friends and remained so until her death. One of the other nurses who greeted us was Sis Featherson, who was the assistant chief nurse at Tripler General Hospital where I was assigned.

While at Tripler, I spent time in the medical, surgical and obstetrical wards. When we had time off, there was plenty to keep us occupied. We went dancing almost every night. I played tennis and went golfing at Fort Shafter. I was having so much fun.

I went AWOL for the first and only time. Elma Asson, one of my nurse friends, was on night duty and wanted me to go in her place with a major from Washington, D.C., on a reconnaissance trip. I approached chief nurse Edna Rockefeller for permission to go on my off day.

"Don't you know better than to come in here and ask to go to the other islands?" she said. "Don't you know that you have to be here six months before you can leave the island of Oahu?"

I started backing out of her office. "No, ma'am, I did not know but thank you for telling me," I replied. I walked out of her office, knowing all along that I was going to go anyway. I took two other nurses with me, including Gelaine Matthews, another of the nurses that I have remained friends with throughout the years.

When we got there, the major went about his business and we visited the islands and had a really good time. When we finally returned to Tripler, we couldn't talk about all of the fun we had because we had been AWOL.

I was on night duty in October, which meant 30 straight days of working from 7 p.m. until 7 a.m. Later, the shift was trimmed to two weeks and we would get either two or three days off. Each night around midnight I would visit my friend Chris Christofferson in the officer's ward for coffee. I remember a good-looking, blond corpsman working on that ward. He had the most beautiful blue eyes and longest black eyelashes I had ever seen on anyone.

One day, I told her I would like to curl his eyelashes and she told me I should bring my eyelash curlers.

Anna and Billy Lappin
in May 1941.

Anna proudly shows off a
snowman she built in Fort
Adams, R.I., March 1941.

"I can't do that," I told her. I didn't know that when we finished night duty that she would ask the corpsman if he would accompany us on a tour of Oahu. But he went with us and we had a nice time touring the island in Chris' car and swimming. At that time Chris was living in a private home and occasionally would invite us out to her house for dinner. It was nice to get away from the hospital atmosphere and often she would do the most beautiful hula to "Hawaiian Sunset" for us. Chris was another of the nurses I stayed in touch with after the war and I visited her in Oakland, California where she lived with her husband.

In November, I was working in the obstetrical ward, which I loved very much. We didn't have too many patients and too many babies. Maybe we had five or six. And in those days, we kept patients in the hospital longer than they do today. They stayed about seven days. While I was working the day shift in the OB ward I discovered something like a pimple on my right cheek. It kept getting bigger and bigger. I tried to treat it myself, but whatever I was doing was not helping. Finally, I reported it to the chief nurse, who immediately diagnosed it as an infection.

I was admitted to the women's ward, located immediately above the maternity ward. I was in the hospital for 10 days or more and the infection was beginning to spread. Dr. Young, chief of medical services at the hospital, suggested that I be transferred back the states for further treatment. Often, infections would heal quicker on the mainland than in the tropics. But I begged Dr. Young to let me stay in Hawaii.

"I'm having such a good time here," I pleaded. "I want to stay here." I guess my persuasion worked because they let me stay. I asked to see a specialist in Honolulu. The specialist suggested that I treat the infection with an antibiotic called sulfa. I was to use sulfa during the day and add a boric acid ointment to the infection at night.

In no time at all, the infection on my cheek began to heal. It probably would have healed without any other treatment, but prior to that they were giving me X-ray treatment and they were giving me something else where I had to use sulfa on my cheek. I was a mess, and what I was worried about the most during that time was the infection was spreading toward my eye and my ear. The whole right cheek was involved, but it was beginning to heal. But I wasn't ready for what was about to happen next.

Chapter Two

December 7: A Day of Infamy

I was still a patient in the women's ward on Dec. 7, 1941. I had just finished eating breakfast and set the tray down on the floor when I heard a terrible noise. Madeline Daugherty, the nurse in charge that morning, ran down the hall. I knew something was wrong, and I ran after her.

We went to the back porch, called a lanai, and we saw smoke spiraling into the sky in the distance. We stood there looking, and a few moments later something flashed before our eyes and hit the oil drum at the pineapple cannery. A big flame went up from the explosion, scaring us something terrible. We ran back into the hall and into Madeline's office. She picked up a phone and called a colonel friend.

"My God," I heard her say, "The Japanese are bombing Pearl Harbor."

When I heard that, I went from being a patient to being a nurse. "I'll be needed on duty," I remember saying. With that, I put on my uniform and reported to the head nurse. I remember starting downstairs with a radio/record player in my arms when I noticed through a window on the obstetrics ward nurse Verla Thompson preparing baby formula.

"The Japanese are bombing Pearl Harbor," I told her.

Verla didn't believe me. She thought that the noise was coming from a military exercise.

"Oh, Anna, you are always kidding," she said. Later that night, Verla assisted two women by delivering their baby boys with only a flashlight for light.

It took only a few minutes for me to make my way to the nurses' quarters. Peggy McKay had a picnic basket on her arm.

"We are celebrating my boyfriend's birthday with a picnic," she said to me.

I quickly ended that notion, telling her what was happening.

"The Japanese are bombing Pearl Harbor and we will all be needed on duty," I said.

I went down the hall to the chief nurse's office, still holding the radio-record player in my arms.

"Where do you think you are going with that red face," she asked me.

"On duty – wherever you need me," I responded.

"I think you better go back to the women's ward and relieve the nurses on duty there. You can't go anywhere with that face looking like that," she said.

I looked like a casualty. I returned to my room, put the radio down and changed my uniform. I was now in charge of the ward where earlier that morning I had been a patient.

Soon, the second wave of Japanese bombers came through. The patients were terrified. I was terrified. Nearly every one of the patients' call lights was on. It was like Broadway – something I'll never forget.

There was one elderly lady on the ward – probably in her 70s or 80s – who reminded me of a pretty Dresden doll with white hair. But she caused a lot of trouble. I heard somebody start yelling, "There's a fire. Nurse, come down."

Sure enough, there was a fire in this lady's room. She had accidentally started a fire with her cigarette. A handkerchief was on fire on the enamel bedside table, so I picked up a pitcher of water and dumped it on the fire. At the same time, I reached for the pack of cigarettes on the bedside stand and grabbed the cigarette that was in her hand. I threw them in a dresser drawer.

"You cannot smoke cigarettes unless someone is with you," I said. "And right now I am alone and do not have time to stay with you." With that, I walked out of the room to begin answering all of the other patients' call lights.

One critically ill patient suffering from abdominal cancer was the quietest of them all. My biggest concern was how to evacuate that patient if it became necessary, but that patient did not require many frequent morphine injections over the next few days.

Everything else from that day is just a blur. I was so busy that I do not remember anything else that happened during the rest of the day. Hectic days followed and I know that I was very scared. That's one thing I'll never forget. Pearl Harbor was the most petrifying experience of my life – it is impossible to forget the first 24 hours.

The corridors of the hospital were overflowing with wounded from Pearl Harbor, many moaning and groaning in agony. Even though all of them already had been injected with morphine, it seemed as if it wasn't enough to quell their pain. It was a horrible sight. The delivery room in the obstetrics ward was converted into an operating room.

When the night nurse came on duty at 7 p.m., I was too frightened to walk to the nurses' quarters, which were located just a short distance away. I was afraid the military police might say, "Halt, who goes there?" and I might be shot because I was too afraid to answer.

That night, I slept in the hospital bed where I had been a patient. I also worked part of the night, relieving the night nurse for an hour while she relieved another nurse on another ward. During the night, I thought of my father, who once told me when I was just a child that a guiding star would always show me the right direction to go. Those thoughts gave me some comfort.

At 6 a.m. on December 8 an enemy plane fired on the dental clinic while the night nurse and I stood on the porch getting some fresh air. We ran inside the hallway and lay on the floor in terror. No one was hurt.

While we were lying on the floor, I silently repeated the Lord's Prayer over and over. The night nurse noticed that I was wearing a rosary. It had been a gift the previous Christmas from Lieutenant Billy Lappin, my old friend in Newport, R.I. We talked about the rosary and Billy, and I told her that I recently had received a letter from him.

"What did he write?" she asked.

I told her that he had ended the letter with a few words in Spanish that I did not understand. He also said that he missed me.

"But what did he say in Spanish?" she asked.

"Y no te olvida. Can you translate that for me, Elma?"

"It means, 'You will never be forgotten,'" Elma said.

How wonderful it was to be thinking of something pleasant, like a sweetheart, who was still thinking of me and wanting to be with me at that very moment. During a terrifying moment such as that, it was a very comforting feeling.

Elma was a devout Catholic and later that month she had my rosary blessed by a priest. I added many religious medals to go along with my rosary, thinking that they all would help. And for many months after Pearl Harbor was bombed, I would touch the cross that was attached to the rosary.

There were plenty of false alarms in the days following the sneak attack on Pearl Harbor. It was always terrifying when the air raid alarm would sound. All of the nurses would run to the basement in the nurses' quarters which was supposed to be the safest place for us to be. We would wait there until the "all clear" was sounded. I always headed straight to the butcher's table, and Madeline Daugherty would tell jokes and keep us laughing until we could leave the basement. I'm not sure if everyone was scared, but I certainly was. I always thought, "This is it."

Later, I heard that Madeline always would take a little sip of whiskey and that was why she would tell jokes.

The air raid alarms continued well into the next year, but after most of them we would always hear the same thing, that friendly ships were approaching the islands.

Tensions were running high across the Hawaiian Islands, and I got to see it first hand. Shortly after the attack a Filipino who was working in the nurses' kitchen and a Japanese kitchen worker began to fight. The Filipino attacked the Japanese worker with a knife, certain that his family in the Philippines was being killed by Japanese soldiers.

There were other scares in addition to the threat of another attack. Two nights after Pearl Harbor was bombed, I heard a commotion in the hallway outside my room around midnight. I saw Madeline, the night supervisor, and asked her what was happening.

"The mattress in the nurses' room caught on fire," she said.

Later I found out that the nurse who started the fire had worked 24 hours straight and was so tired that she had fallen asleep with a cigarette in her hand.

Elma and I were in charge of supplies in the triage room where the wounded were sorted by the gravity of their injuries. The more seriously wounded were taken to surgery first. Elma and I checked the triage to make sure all of the supplies were in place and that nothing was touched.

Gas and food were rationed in the days following the attack. Food stores were closed for a day for inventory. There was a ban placed on all liquor sales and the bars and saloons were closed. Three Japanese banks in Honolulu were closed. Japanese nationals were placed under strict control and regulations. Everybody was on edge. The military was certain that the Japanese would attack again.

In an effort to prevent profiteering, which always happens in wartime, and to regulate the issuance of staples, a military governor ordered all firearms held by individuals to be surrendered, except those with special authority to carry them for defense purposes.

General Walter Short announced that the Japanese air raiders had shot down the Army flag on December 7. He also cited seven Army flyers with shooting down several enemy planes.

In 1942 the nurses who served during and after the attack on Pearl Harbor received a Presidential citation.

"You are the Bravest of the Brave with a devotion to duty and to mankind that will be forever unmatched," the citation read. It was signed by President Franklin Delano Roosevelt.

Secretary of the Navy Knox arrived in Hawaii to investigate the Pearl Harbor attack and he returned to Washington on Dec. 13. Shortly after his return, military authorities announced the first restrictions on gasoline consumption by using a card-rationing system.

One of our nurses, Blanche Kiernan, had a Chevrolet that seemed to always be in need of some type of repair. We gave her the nickname 'Shasta' because 'She has ta' always have some repairs done. Blanche always was able to get gasoline to take us on little tours on our off-days, and that was a lot of fun.

Several months later, I was out on a date with an officer. As we were driving home, a Japanese man who I'm certain must have been drunk, jumped onto the jeep. We swerved almost into the ditch before my officer friend managed to punch him. We hurried home, and I never rode in an open vehicle again.

I met my future husband, Sherrill, in 1943 and our courtship lasted through 1944. We met after I received a promotion, and I was at Lanikai for some R and R – rest and recreation. There was a lovely place on the beach for all of the officers. It was lunchtime on a Saturday and Sherrill was seated across the table from me. Sherrill, a second lieutenant, mentioned that he had played football with the Brooklyn Dodgers and was a graduate of Troy State Teacher's College. Even though I had lived in Brooklyn and knew of the baseball team, I didn't know there was a football team named the Dodgers.

That night, a movie was being shown in the recreation room. After it was over, Sherrill approached me and asked if he could buy me a Coca-Cola.

I said, “No thank you,” and returned to my room in the other quarters.

The next morning I was sitting alone on the beach when Sherrill came by.

“What is a pretty girl like you doing out here on the beach alone?” he asked.

“Waiting for you,” I said.

We went swimming together and became better acquainted. I told him that I had just been promoted to first lieutenant and to chief nurse even though I was still at Tripler for orientation.

I needed a ride back to the nurses' quarters, but Sherrill was Officer of the Day, which meant that he would be on duty beginning at 4 p.m.

“I'll take you back,” he said. I'll get transportation for you.”

Sherrill, who was in special services, was stationed at Bellows Field, which was a long, long block from the beach. He went back to the base, found somebody else to be OD, and came back for me in a jeep. He drove me back to Tripler, which was about 20 miles away.

I remember riding along in the jeep and singing a lot of popular songs together. We sang songs like, “A Pretty Girl is Like a Pretty

Melody," and "Smile Awhile." We also sang, "Someone Like You, A Pal So Good and True," and "Let the Rest of the World Go By."

When we walked into the nurses' quarters at Tripler, Sherrill immediately saw the piano that was about 20 feet away from the door in our huge living room. I thought it was strange when he walked over to the piano, but he sat down and just started playing. I just sat there and listened.

After a while, he came over to where I was sitting. We sat there and talked for a long time until he had to leave.

From then on, we were constant companions. We played golf and swam together. I went to baseball and football games, and we just had a wonderful time together. Sherrill usually would come over to the Fort Shafter Golf Course, which was located across from the nurses' quarters. Usually, I would be over there playing alone. Sherrill was an excellent golfer, but his best sports were baseball, football and tennis. He used to tell me that golf was a sissy's game, but that didn't stop him from giving me a nice little necklace with a golfer on it.

As our relationship grew, Sherrill proposed to me on several occasions. Each time, however, I told him that I wasn't ready to marry. He knew that there was somebody on the mainland that I was interested in.

That somebody was Billy Lappin, my old friend back in Newport, R.I. His letters were lovely and I still have some of them today. I wrote to Billy in May, 1944 that I was thinking of getting married. Of course, it seems that all of my letters to him probably made him feel like I was dating everyone else and that I was probably losing interest in him, so he didn't write to me as frequently.

In May, Sherrill made clear his intentions.

"I want to give you your engagement ring, and I want you to go back to the States and see that old boyfriend," he said. "If you decide that you would rather marry him than me, you keep the ring and marry him."

I thought about his proposition for quite awhile and even sent Billy a letter. I told him that I was going to request a leave and asked if he would meet me in New York. He answered back, saying that he would meet me there.

May, June and July went by and I still hadn't received my leave. Sherrill came to visit me at my Kaneohe office in early August, shortly after I had received permission to go on leave.

"Well, when are you going on that leave to the mainland," he inquired.

We sat and talked awhile. I showed him the leave and he handed it back to me. My leave was scheduled for September. Instead, I tore it up in front of him. It was my answer to his marriage proposal.

Often when we went to town we would stop by various jewelry stores. We'd look at rings, and Sherrill wanted me to select the exact ring that I wanted. But I didn't want to.

"I'm not interested in big diamonds," I told him. "One little diamond will be fine." .

Two weeks before we were married, he gave me an engagement ring. Fourteen months after we first met, we were married in the Fort Shafter Chapel. The date was September 16, 1944.

Only about a dozen friends were invited to our wedding. Alma Eidsaa was my maid of honor. Tom Winsett, who played for the Boston Red Sox, was our best man. He, Sherrill and Joe DiMaggio (yes, that Joe DiMaggio of the mighty New York Yankees) all played for the 7th Air Force team, known as the Pacific Powerhouse.

We honeymooned right there in Honolulu at the Halekulani Hotel, one of the three best hotels on the island along with the Royal Hawaiian and the Young Hotel. After the ceremony, champagne was served. Somebody said something about a football or baseball game the next day. I remember telling Sherrill that we should go watch it.

After we were married, I stayed at the nurses' quarters and Sherrill stayed at his quarters.

Eventually, a detective friend of ours rented us his small apartment on Waikiki Beach. We were half a block from the water.

In 1945 I was assigned to the Farrington area, a school that had been converted into a hospital. I continued my duties as chief area nurse until later that year. While I was at Farrington, the war finally came to an end when the U.S. dropped two atomic bombs on the Japanese mainland.

When we heard that the war was over, we were all very jubilant. I don't know how to describe it except that everybody got very happy. I called Sherrill when I found out and he had heard the news, too. It was a wonderful time. In September, 1945, I left Hawaii on a three-month leave.

Anna with a baby delivered
at Tripler, 1942.

Anna with her brother, Stephen Urda, her cousin,
Marie Urda, and her nurse friend.

Chapter Three

Homeward Bound

After a couple of mix-ups, my orders were finally straightened out and I was given my choice of reporting to either Northington General Hospital or another hospital in Daytona Beach, Fla. I opted for Northington General Hospital in Tuscaloosa. I was assigned to the medical surgical ward at Northington. It was different from anything that I had been accustomed to because there was a great influx of military personnel returning home. Our ward was like a convalescent ward. It was unlike anything I had ever dealt with in my career.

During my early days at Northington, Sherrill was making his way back home. On December 16, I had a telegram from him that he had been assigned to Camp Shelby. I requested a short leave as soon as I found out when Sherrill would be arriving in Tuscaloosa. We met at the Tuscaloosa station. I was so happy to see him. We both were in uniform and I think everybody on the train was looking at this nurse and officer running to greet each other.

Sherrill was discharged from the military on January 16, 1946. At the same time, I was scheduled to have surgery for a saphenous ligation on my left leg.

After the surgery, Sherrill came to Tuscaloosa and I was granted a 30-day leave. We took the train to Pennsylvania, New York and Washington, D.C., to visit family and friends.

While in Washington D.C., we took time out to visit the Pentagon. I met with Colonel Florence A. Blanchfield, who was the chief of the Army Nurse Corps. I expressed to her how much I enjoyed my seven years in the nurse corps.

Sherrill and I were eager to get settled. We were planning to enroll at the University of Alabama. Sherrill wanted to earn a masters and Ph.D. I told Colonel Blanchfield that I wanted to continue nursing and that I would like to be transferred to Maxwell Field. My husband's family lived near there, I told her, and I wanted to get to know them better.

Before leaving, Colonel Blanchfield told me to request a transfer as soon as I returned to Northington.

"Do it immediately and it will be granted within 30 days," she told me.

I did, and that's exactly what happened - I was transferred to Maxwell Army Air Field Hospital.

While Sherrill was studying at Alabama, I spent as much time with his family as I could. I would get on the bus and go for a visit every chance I had.

There always was plenty of love in the Busby family. In the spring -March and April -I noticed that Papa Busby would sometimes sit out on the porch and Mama would always bring him a cup of coffee at a certain time each afternoon. Other times, Papa Busby would simply say to his wife, "Annie, you are the prettiest woman in this world." Of course, she would always kiss him before leaving on the bus to shop at the Montgomery Fair.

While I was at Maxwell Field, the chief nurse told me that I had too much leave built up and that I was in danger of losing some of it if I didn't use it. After discussing it with Sherrill, I decided to resign from military service. I had accumulated four months of leave, so technically I didn't leave the military until August 29,1946.

I enrolled at the university with Sherrill, taking home economics classes first and then nursing courses. Sherrill's family wanted him to complete his education, coach awhile, and then settle down.

When the summer session was over, Sherrill surprised me. On this late August day, we went to breakfast. I had been working in conjunction with the Red Cross to find a place for us to live if we were going to continue our education at Alabama. After breakfast, Sherrill told me to go up to our room and wait. I thought we were going to move into a new apartment, but Sherrill had other plans.

"We've got to re-pack everything," he said. "I've just taken a job. We're moving to Pine Bluff, Arkansas."

It was the first of many surprises I would encounter during the remainder of my married life.

"Where are we going to live," I asked Sherrill.

"Don't worry," he replied. "It's all settled. We're going to live right next to the high school. Coach Terry, the head football coach, has arranged for a very nice furnished apartment for us."

We left Tuscaloosa for a short stay in Montgomery. From there, it was on to Pine Bluff.

Chapter Four

Sherrill Busby

I didn't know everything about Sherrill until after we were married. I knew he played football at Troy State and that he had played for the Brooklyn Dodgers. When we met in Hawaii, it wasn't love at first sight. Sherrill didn't drink and didn't smoke -there were only about three men in my life who didn't. I knew that I didn't want to marry anyone who did. Oh, a few cocktails were OK, but nobody who was a heavy drinker.

In Hawaii, we saw each other at least once a week and sometimes a couple of times a week. Sherrill's schedule was busy, as was mine. But we did what we could to get time together.

Sherrill was a good athlete. He was playing on the 7th Air Force baseball team. Usually, he would invite me to the games on the weekend. One time, he made reservations for me to sit near the press box. Sherrill told me before the game that he would look for me in the crowd, and when he saw me, he'd bend down to tie his shoelace. I thought that was sweet.

We enjoyed each other's company very much, but I didn't want him to take me for granted. One time, he didn't invite me to the game. We were walking down a street in Honolulu, and we were fussing. Sherrill asked me what was wrong.

"You didn't invite me to your game," I said.

"I thought you knew that you had a standing invitation to all my games," he replied.

Well, I went to the game that Saturday and to every other one that I was able to make it to.

Because there were so few women in Hawaii, dates were always easy to come by. But after awhile, I didn't care about going out with anyone else. I was having a lot of fun with Sherrill. There wasn't anything we couldn't talk about. It didn't matter if I had any more dates or not. I had found the person that I wanted to be with.

Sherrill always knew our marriage was "until death do us part." Today, it seems like so many people go through two or three marriages. Not ours. I was attracted to Sherrill for so many reasons. He was witty and entertaining. He had a great sense of humor and was very talented.

He could play the organ and the piano. He could play the drums and the harmonica. He was a coach and a teacher. He knew all about drama and he was a ventriloquist. There was so much to love about him.

Before enlisting in the service, Sherrill played one year of football with the Dodgers. But he got hurt, and that was the end of his professional career. I don't think he ever regretted only getting to play that one year, though. At that time, it didn't matter who you were -you went into the service. Sherrill always wanted to be a coach, anyway. He love being around children, and children loved being around him. It seemed as though everybody loved him. I used to joke with him that children were his No.1 priority, and I was his No.2 priority.

Sherrill loved magic and we attended the International Magician's Show in Chicago. He had a magic act that he would perform to help children raise funds for their various schools. They would charge 25 cents for a 30-minute performance and the audience would sit back in delight as Sherrill dazzled them with card tricks or handkerchief tricks. Most of the tricks were sleight-of-hand, and he could make the handkerchief dance and flirt, run and hide, and appear and disappear.

It seemed like whenever a group of people were at our home or gathered in public, Sherrill would say, "Pick a card." He never stopped at one or two tricks. Someone always was asking him to turn up a card or to cover a card.

He also performed at the Linden Plantation Country Club. He had all sorts of tricks -with his silk high hats, with an umbrella, with a cigar, with cigarettes and with eggs. In one of the most popular tricks Sherrill was

THE NATIONAL FOOTBALL LEAGUE

UNIFORM PLAYER'S CONTRACT

The BROOKLYN DODGERS FOOTBALL CLUB, Inc. herein called the Club,

and Sherrill Busby of Alabama herein called the Player.

The Club is a member of The National Football League. As such, and jointly with the other members of the League, it is obligated to insure to the public wholesome and high-class professional football by defining the relations between Club and Player, and between Club and Club.

In view of the facts above recited the parties agree as follows:

1. The Club will pay the Player a salary for his skilled services during the playing season of 1940, at the rate of See Below dollars for each regularly scheduled League game played. For all other games the Player shall be paid such salary as shall be agreed upon between the Player and the Club. As to games scheduled but not played, the Player shall receive no compensation from the Club other than actual expenses. The Club will pay the Player One Hundred Dollars per game for the first three games, and One Hundred Fifteen Dollars per game for the remaining games...The Club will furnish the Player with Transportation from his home to the Training camp.

2. The salary above provided for shall be paid by the Club as follows:

Seventy-five per cent (75%) after each game and the remaining twenty-five per cent (25%) at the close of the season or upon release of the Player by the Club.

3. The Player agrees that during said season he will faithfully serve the Club, and pledges himself to the American public to conform to high standards of fair play and good sportsmanship.

4. The Player will not play football during 1940 otherwise than for the Club, except in case the Club shall have released said Player, and said release has been approved by the officials of The National Football League.

5. **The Player will not participate in an exhibition game after the completion of the schedule of the Club and prior to August 1 of the following season, without the permission of the President of the League.**

6. The Player accepts as part of this contract such reasonable regulations as the Club may announce from time to time.

7. This contract may be terminated at any time by the club giving notice in writing to the player within forty-eight (48) hours after the day of the last game in which he is to participate with his club.

8. The Player submits himself to the discipline of The National Football League and agrees to accept its decisions pursuant to its Constitution and By-Laws.

9. Any time prior to August 1st, 1941, by written notice to the Player, the Club may renew this contract for the term of that year, except that the salary rate shall be such as the parties may then agree upon, or in default of agreement, such as the Club may fix.

the "Jack and the Beanstalk." He used a milk pitcher and a newspaper. When he rolled it up and cut it a certain way it would look like a ladder. As he was doing all of this, he would be telling the story of Jack and the Beanstalk. Children and adults loved it. I also enjoyed his trick where he would pull a rabbit out of a high hat.

Sherrill often told me I was a bossy person. He said I was always telling him to do this and to do that. He simply would tell me to leave him a note on the refrigerator what to do and he'd get to it when he could. But that was just his way.

When I'd come home, he'd have done everything I'd asked and usually more. Sherrill told me one time that if I had stayed in the military, I would have ended up being a general. I said no, but I probably would have been a colonel. Sherrill was always busy teaching school and coaching. Sometimes I'd help him grade papers, but it wasn't tough being a coach's wife back then. I was always so busy. He was always saying that I was too busy. He said one day I'd be dead and still have too much to do.

Sherrill received his master's degree in 1949 from the University of Alabama and in May 1950 was in the gym and began feeling sick. He came home and told me that he didn't feel well. He went to see the doctor that afternoon and was admitted to the Davis Hospital suffering from coronary insufficiency.

Dr. Monroe, the attending physician, told me what I could expect with Sherrill's condition.

"With this type of diagnosis, you never know," he said. "He could die suddenly or he could live for a long time."

It took about two weeks for Sherrill to recover. His second EKG showed improvement and the third was completely normal, which was very strange. The doctors told him he couldn't coach for the rest of the year. He got a second opinion from two other doctors. One doctor in Memphis said he could coach if he wanted to.

After he recovered from his heart condition, Sherrill had several jobs. He conducted study hall for a while and also sold vacuum cleaners. Later, he accepted a job in the small town of Gould, which was about 30 miles from Pine Bluff. I didn't really want to move to that little town, but their football team hadn't been doing very well and Sherrill wanted the challenge to make them better. By the second season, the team won three games, but Sherrill still wasn't happy. He told me he didn't think the team was doing well enough. I told him he was being silly.

"Two years ago, the team didn't win a game and now they've won three. That's improvement," I said.

Sherrill was always looking out for the children. When it came time for graduation, there was one girl in the senior class who wasn't allowed to go dancing. After the graduation ceremony, there was going to be a dance. Sherrill had organized the party, and it had a Hawaiian theme. But the parents of this girl weren't going to let her go to graduation exercises or the dance. Sherrill wanted to make sure she was allowed to attend. He and I went to the girl's home and asked her parents to let her attend. He told them we would be there the whole evening and that we wouldn't let her dance.

We assured them we would bring her straight home after it was over. To Sherrill's delight, the girl's parents consented and let her go to graduation. It seemed as though Sherrill was always doing something like that for his students.

Eventually, Sherrill accepted a job at Highland Home High School near Montgomery in 1957 and we moved back to Alabama.

Sherrill drove back and forth to Highland Home. It was a short commute and he didn't seem to mind it at all. Shortly after we returned to Alabama, Sherrill and I bought a lake home on a four-acre island at Lake Martin. It was just three rooms, but we fell in love with it after renting it one weekend. When we got home from our weekend away, Sherrill looked at me and said, "Let's buy that place at the lake."

Sherrill told me to get the man who owned it on the phone, and that's exactly what I did. The owner told us to meet him and his attorney the next morning and we would talk about the sale. We did, and we bought it. I kept that lake home for 18 years. Sherrill and I enjoyed that lake house. It was cute, and I mean cute.

We spent a lot of time there. If I didn't go up on the weekend, he would go up. It was our own little getaway. Sherrill didn't want a television, phone or a radio up there, and it wasn't until later that I added some of those things. I loved picking flowers up there. I went swimming all the time. He always wanted to take poor children who didn't have the means to swim and fish up there, and that's what he did. Sherrill wanted to enlarge our lake house. He wanted to put in a screened-in porch. Before he died, he was making a sandbox for children to play in. I asked him what children?

He only said, "You'll see."

Later, I carried out his wishes.

In early 1960, Sherrill wanted me to quit my job at Maxwell Air Force Base. His plan was for us to buy more houses and rent them out.

I said, "Sherrill, who is going to take care of painting, plumbing and anything else that happened?"

He told me not to worry about it. Sherrill always was a man of action. We wanted to buy a boat and an organ for our home, so I made a deal with Sherrill.

"Those are costly things," I told him. "I promise that I will quit my job before Thanksgiving or Christmas. But if I work until then, we'll be able to have a boat and an organ before I quit."

Not only was Sherrill a man of action, he was always full of surprises. Sherrill seemed to always surprise me with something - either birthday parties or dinner parties. One day I came home and he had invited a bunch of our friends over for a picnic. Steaks were cooking on the grill and we had a house full of friends. Another time he bought me makeup that I didn't use and wine that he didn't drink for my birthday.

In April 1960, he came in the house one day and told me to look out the window. I did, and sitting in the driveway was a new four-door Chevrolet. That was my husband. You never knew what he was going to do. When he died, I was concerned about how I would pay for this new car. But even in death, Sherrill found a way to surprise me. Later, I found out that he had taken out insurance when he bought the car. When he died, the insurance covered the cost of the car.

He also insisted that we have a weekly maid and a gardener. He never wanted me to mow the front yard because "It's not something Southern women do." But he did let me mow the back yard because nobody could see me. He also would hire someone to cook and wash dishes whenever we entertained friends.

The day Sherrill died, June 7, 1960, we were at William Spear's house near the lake home. They were good friends of ours, and Sherrill was teaching their 4-year-old son to ski. Sherrill was always doing something like that.

I was on the pier watching them. Sherrill was in the water.

"Anna, come get me," he yelled.

I wondered what kind of prank he was pulling on me this time. But those were his last words to me.

It didn't take long to see that he was in trouble. Virginia Spear jumped into the water, and she and I were able to pull him onto the shore. We immediately began to try to resuscitate him.

A lot of what happened that day is still a blur. There were two ministers on the shore and we jumped into somebody's car. I remember saying, "Just get us to a hospital."

I guess I went into a nursing mode because when we got to the hospital, I started yelling, "Adrenaline and oxygen. Adrenaline and oxygen."

The staff asked me to leave the room, and it wasn't long before the doctor came out and gave me the news.

"Mrs. Busby, your husband died instantly," he said.

I refused to believe him. "My husband is not dead," I told him.

I went into the room where he was lying and felt for a pulse.

"I feel a pulse," I said.

He shook his head. "Mrs. Busby, your husband is dead."

At that time I went into shock. I remember riding back to Montgomery with Virginia. She gave me a piece of paper and asked me to write down everyone that needed to be contacted. I did, and she took care of it.

The next few days and weeks are still a blur. I couldn't believe Sherrill was dead.

Life after Sherrill's death wasn't easy. I was uncertain about the future. How would I support myself? What would I do without him? After spending 17 years with a person, it's not easy to wake up one day and not have them there.

Chapter Five

Life on My Own

As had been the case all my life, I immersed myself in my work. I returned to work at Maxwell in June. It was too early for me to get back to work. And although everybody was wonderful to me, I still was grieving the loss of Sherrill. The healing process was long and drawn out. It took me several years to get over my grief.

Finally, I resigned from Maxwell Air Force base in October 1961, when I found out I could make ends meet from all of the rental properties we owned. And I returned to the University of Alabama to continue my nursing studies. But in 1963, I had another life-altering event. I went to the doctor for a checkup and it revealed an ovarian cyst. I went for a second opinion, but the diagnosis was the same. Shortly thereafter, I underwent surgery.

Following the surgery, I returned to Montgomery and returned to private duty nursing. I remained in the private sector for a little more than two years.

In 1966, I went to work for the state of Alabama on the tuberculosis program. I was headquartered in Florence and sometimes made rounds with nurses when they were having trouble getting patients admitted into the sanitariums.

Between 1967 and 1969, I worked on the Inactive Health Personnel Project (IHPP), commissioned by the U.S. Public Health Service

Department. At that time, there was a shortage of nurses nationwide, and this project was a refresher course to update nurses who hadn't worked in five years or more. I became involved in the project almost by accident. A nurse friend of mine called me about a six-week class for nurse aids. The cost was $80. When I arrived to see what the course was about, I was flabbergasted. It was a fly-by-night operation. When I saw what was going on, I went straight to Mrs. Walter Bragg Smith, who was the state's project director. I showed her the outline from the fly-by-night organization, and after a series of phone calls, she offered me a job coordinating the IHPP. I taught several classes, and by the time the project ended in 1969, 71 percent of the nurses in Alabama who took the course were still working either full- or part-time two years later.

In 1969, I had heard about the Pearl Harbor Survivors Association from a nurse friend of mine. At that time, Alabama didn't have a chapter. I traveled to a district convention in Atlanta and later to others in Washington, D.C., and New York. I met several of the chapter presidents, including Hank Shane, the national president. He and I talked, and he told me that one of his goals was to include nurses in the membership. At that time, the organization, like many others, was comprised primarily of men, even though there were a good number of nurses who had been at Pearl Harbor.

I decided to organize a chapter in Montgomery, and I placed a notice in the newspaper. To be recognized by the national Pearl Harbor Survivors Association, we needed at least seven people to sign up.

Hank came down on a whim to see what I was doing. I presided at the meeting, which drew about 20 people. After the meeting, Hank wanted to put me in charge of organizing the nurses and to give me a title. The name we came up with was National Chairperson, White Caps, and I've held the position ever since. I took the job to heart. Whenever I was traveling, I would make sure to call nurses in the area and ask them to join. Within a year, I had recruited 60 nurses to the membership.

I've attended nearly every national convention since, including three trips to Hawaii, Las Vegas, California, Virginia, Florida and other states. At the conventions, we don't talk much about the war. The conventions are mostly fun and there is a lot of friendship among the members. It's important we keep future generations informed about war.

Becoming an active member in PHSA, I was able to renew friendships with many of the men and women I served with at Pearl Harbor, and I also made many new friends. My work with the PHSA is something I'm very proud of. I think the organization has done an excellent job of maintaining awareness about what happened that Sunday morning, December 7,1941, and, hopefully, ensuring that nothing like it will ever happen again.

In the early 1970s, I decided to write "White Cap Sketches," a collection of memoirs from nurses who were stationed at Pearl Harbor on December 7, 1941. To do that, I attempted to contact all of the nurses who were stationed at Pearl Harbor that day. I asked them to write their testimonials about what they were doing precisely at 7:55 a.m. the morning of the attack. Twenty-six nurses responded and I used eight of their testimonials. I had it published and took it to the Pearl Harbor Survivors Association (PHSA) convention that year in Pearl Harbor. Although I had a limited number of copies, all of them sold during a 15-minute coffee break at the convention. I made a total of $400 and promptly wrote a check for $365 to the Sons and Daughters of Pearl Harbor Survivors Association so that the group would have some money.

I think I've always loved to write. I always was able to immerse myself in writing. It was something that I took great pride in and it allowed me to express some of my feelings.

When Sherrill was alive, I talked about writing my autobiography and he always said he would help me with it. After I became widowed, I put the project on hold because I was very busy with other things. Nursing took up a lot of my time, but I always managed to join literary and writing groups.

It seems as though I was never able to slow down for any length of time. I was either working or traveling throughout the 1970s and 1980s.

In 1970, St. Jude's Hospital in Montgomery wanted to start a continuing education program. Sister Evangeline, a friend of mine for many years, was the head nun at the hospital. She begged me to organize the program so they could pass their accreditation.

I knew what needed to be done, and I knew some other nurses at other hospitals who were enrolled in some continuing education classes. One day, Sister Evangeline arranged for me to meet with the hospital administrator to discuss the program. I spent the next six months setting up the continuing education program at the hospital. After that, the hospital easily passed its accreditation.

While I was at St. Jude, two black women were admitted to the hospital. Both of them were pregnant and were scheduled to deliver their babies by caesarean section. I was told that each of the women had been pregnant between 12 and 16 times. I was astonished by this fact.

Their C-sections were both done at night, and the doctor who performed them tied their tubes so they could not get pregnant again.

The incident reminded me of what Sherrill told me in the past, "A Yankee will have a hard time understanding the area's culture. Unless you are from the South, you will never understand it." I think after that night, I began to fully understand what he meant.

For two years in the 1980s, I worked with Meals on Wheels delivering meals around the neighborhood. I also served as a board member for the YMCA, Alabama Nurses Association, American Security Council and the Listerhill Clinic. I worked with the Retired Army Nurses Corps Association (RANCA), and I was involved with the Alabama Regional Library for the Blind and Physically Handicapped for nearly 10 years. I've also been inducted into the Maxwell Air Force Base Hall of Fame.

I was even involved with the Gulf War. I worked with the Red Cross at Maxwell Air Force Base taking blood pressures. I also became an active participant in the Women in Military Service for America Memorial foundation's project to build a women's memorial in Washington D.C. by providing the organization with many names of the nurses who served at Pearl Harbor.

The groundbreaking for the memorial was held in 1997, and I was able to visit it in April 2001. It contains a computer database for every woman who served in the military since the American Revolution. The memorial is something we should all be proud of.

In the past few years, the attack on Pearl Harbor has gained a good deal of attention. In December 2000, several people contacted me about a National Geographic documentary that was being filmed in conjunction with a movie that was about to be released in the summer. At first, a representative of WIMSA (Women in Military Service Association) asked if I would consent to an interview for the documentary. Later, a person from NPR called and we arranged for the interview to be taped on February 15, 2001.

A film crew from New York arrived at my home to record the interview. I had to apply all sorts of makeup, and I had to be dressed just right. They came into my house, and I just told them to do whatever they needed to do to get ready.

The interview lasted nearly four hours. I was asked all kinds of questions by the interviewer, but one thing they seemed to want to focus on was the romantic aspect of life at Pearl Harbor. I told them as much as I could remember, but I'm not really sure why they were so interested in that part of the story.

I also gave them access to as much of my collection of memorabilia as they wanted. I told them to take anything they wanted. My only request was that they give me a copy of my entire interview, which they did. It's on four videocassette tapes.

I enjoyed every bit of it, and I received a lot of attention for my part in the documentary, which is called "Pearl Harbor and Beyond." It aired in May 2001. Some people have told me I'm a celebrity, but I don't feel like one. All I did was my job at Pearl Harbor.

Epilogue

I am reminded almost daily that there is still much to do to keep our country safe and free. I had just finished breakfast on Sept. 11 and was about to carry my tray back into the kitchen. I had the television on when the first news of attacks on the World Trade Center and Pentagon came on. It brought back many memories of Dec. 7, 1941, the morning Pearl Harbor was attacked by the Japanese. That morning I also had just finished eating breakfast and put my tray down when the attack occurred.

This day, I felt as though I needed to be with someone. I left home for the Great Books classes at the Archibald Center in downtown Montgomery. I noticed a very blue sky and that there were few cars on the road.

In December 2001, I had the privilege of returning to Hawaii to help commemorate the 60th anniversary of Japan's sneak attack on Pearl Harbor. The Pearl Harbor Survivors Association held its annual convention in Honolulu in conjunction with the anniversary, and in attendance were over 2,000 survivors and their families.

Mary Jane Ellis, a retired military friend, traveled with me. Mary Jane and I began our journey west early on the morning of Dec. 4 when we boarded a Delta Airlines jet in Montgomery. Flying time was 10 hours, but the trip took much longer because of various layovers in Atlanta and Los Angeles along the way. Also, security was tight in the aftermath of the events of Sept. 11, when terrorists staged their own sneak attack on the World Trade Center and Pentagon.

I was given red-carpet treatment along the way, and was overjoyed when our pilot on the flight to Atlanta made this announcement: "We have a celebrity on board. Mrs. Anna Urda Busby is a Pearl Harbor Survivor nurse." On each flight the rest of the way, pilots made the same announcement. It made me proud to have served our country.

The anticipation of a memorable week grew with each passing minute. When our plane finally touched down in Hawaii, I was finally back in my own paradise. Jet lag may take its toll on some, but not on a 90-year-old ex-nurse returning to the site of some of her most vivid memories.

Much of our first day involved registering for the convention, and that involved plenty of waiting in long lines. Fortunately, Mary Jane did much of the waiting while I took time to renew friendships and make new ones.

That night, we were feted with an authentic Polynesian performance and dinner.

On Dec. 6, Mary Jane and I explored many of the places that hold special memories. Our first stop was Kamehameha School atop one of the mountains overlooking Honolulu. The site is as spectacular today as it was in 1941. During the war, many of the buildings were converted into a hospital. I was excited to find the same buildings, and delighted when I rediscovered the nurses' quarters.

We rode around the Fort Shafter Military Reservations and Tripler Army Medical Center where I was stationed on Dec. 7th. Our last stop was a visit to Hickam Air Force Base. Everywhere I went I was welcomed with hugs and kisses, and I was interviewed countless times by the media.

The trip became more solemn on Dec. 7 when we traveled to the Punchbowl, the National Memorial Cemetery of the Pacific, for a ceremony commemorating the attack on Pearl Harbor and to remember our fallen heroes. Representatives of the New York City firefighters and police department attended. Gen. Richard Myers of the Joint Chiefs of Staff and Robin Higgins, Under Secretary for Memorial Affairs in the Department of Veterans Affairs delivered keynote speeches.

Anna returning to Hawaii for the 60th Anniversary of the attack on Pearl Harbor, December 2001.

Top and left: Anna re-visits Kamehameha Schools, December 2001.

That night, Sam Donaldson of ABC News was the featured speaker at a banquet for the convention visitors. Everybody dressed in Aloha attire. It was a day in which everybody reminisced about our country's past and its future, and to reflect on the Pearl Harbor Survivors Association's motto: "Remember Pearl Harbor – Keep America Alert!"

I finally had some free time on our final day in Hawaii. Mary Jane and I spent six hours exploring Oahu. I took many pictures while visiting many of the same places Sherrill and I had visited when we were stationed there. The day brought back hundreds of fond memories from happier times. Although this wasn't the first time I had returned to Hawaii, it has grown so much over the years. Sometimes, it seemed I wasn't even sure that it was the same place.

The day did yield one pleasant surprise. I phoned a friend from World War II, Mun Charn Wong, whose wedding Sherrill and I attended during the war. We had a pleasant conversation, and it was a great way to wrap up an unforgettable week.

It was with reluctance that we headed for the airport on Dec. 9 for our journey home.

"I could have stayed another week or two. There was so much more to see and do," I remarked to Mary Jane.

We landed in Montgomery early on the morning of Dec. 10. I was elated that I had not missed the reunion, but sad that the week had gone by so quickly. And I was grateful that I had been able to see all of my old friends again.

These days, I am busy promoting my book and enjoy numerous speaking engagements.

I am troubled by recent world events in Afghanistan and the Middle East. I wonder what it all means, and if the world learned nothing from the lessons of World War II. I worry that it hasn't.

It's been a very enjoyable life. Of course, like everybody else, it's had plenty of ups and downs. I have enjoyed meeting people of all cultures, and I think that is because of my background as a nurse.

I don't have any regrets. No problems have arisen that I couldn't somehow find a way to solve. I've contributed to society on the national, state, city and community levels. I think if I could do it all over again, I would probably do it the same way. I only wish that Sherrill had been around to share the past 40 years with me. To this day, I still miss him. When we married, I guess I hoped that we would both live well into our 70s. Sherrill knew that when we were married it would be forever.

Still, I have been very, very lucky in many respects. I think if half the people in the world would be as happy as I have been, then we'd have a very happy world to live in.

I've enjoyed reflecting on my life the past few years. When you reach my age, what else do you have except for your memories?

Anna, December 2006, at the 65th Anniversary Symposium held in Waikiki, Hawaii.

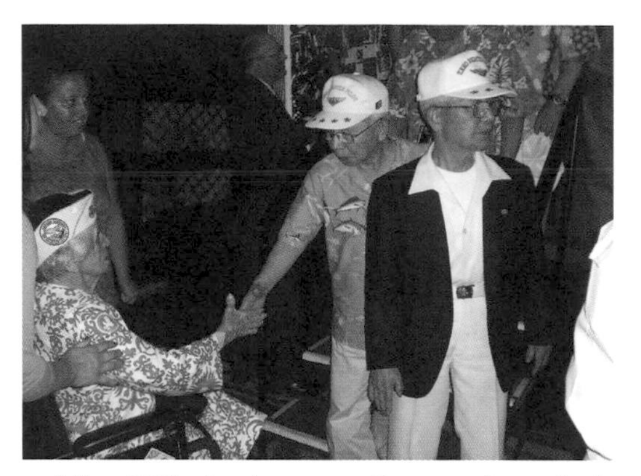

Above: Anna at the 65th Anniversary Symposium shakes hands with Japanese pilots who participated in the bombing of Pearl Harbor. Anna told them, "God forgives you and so do I. Now we must get along and love one another."

Left: Anna speaks at the 65th Anniversary Symposium in Waikiki, December 2006, with her niece, Kathryn Shust.

Anna and her family in Hawaii for the 65th Anniversary, December 2006
Front row: Daria Endler, Anna, Kathryn Shust. Back row: Bruce Endler, Lillian Shust, Stephen Shust Jr.

Excerpts from

White Cap Sketches

Anna Danyo Willgrube

The little town of Jermyn, one of the smallest in the state of Pennsylvania, is located in the northern part of the Pocono Mountains right in the heart of the anthracite coal region. A small river, the Lackawanna, runs through town and is the only link to the ocean. Yet there was something about the open sea that appealed to me and I longed to make an ocean voyage.

Nursing became my chosen profession after I helped nurse a younger sister following a serious car accident. After I completed high school I was accepted as a student at the Pennsylvania Hospital in Philadelphia. This hospital has the distinction of being the first hospital established as a hospital in the United States and was built in 1751. At the end of three years, I decided to specialize in operating room supervision and applied to Johns Hopkins Hospital in Baltimore, Maryland, for the four month course they offered. Upon completion, I returned to the Pennsylvania Hospital and served as assistant operating room supervisor for two years when I accepted a more lucrative position in Easton, Maryland as operating room supervisor. However, after three years, I decided it was time to "go to sea". War was imminent in Europe and I was approaching the age limit for entering.

I applied for a commission in the Navy Nurse Corps and was sworn in on January 29, 1940; my first duty station was U.S. Naval Hospital,

Washington D.C., the present site of the Navy's Bureau of Medicine and Surgery. I served for eighteen months and decided to make Navy Nursing my career. My joy was boundless when I received orders to the newly commissioned hospital ship, the U.S.S. Solace, a most enviable assignment on my first transfer. I reported for duty on the Solace in August, 1941. After a shakedown cruise, we sailed to Norfolk, Virginia, then through the Panama Canal to Long Beach, California, before we finally sailed for Pearl Harbor. We arrived at Pearl Harbor on October 27, 1941.

Since I was the most junior nurse on board, I was assigned relief duty. I relieved each nurse as she took her turn on night duty. The weekend of December 6 and 7, 1941, I was assigned afternoon duty on a surgical ward. That Saturday afternoon, a group of nurses from the Solace and the local Naval Hospital took a hike and I joined the group for part of the hike. It was interesting despite the blisters on my heels and toes. I had not noticed anything unusual but we did notice natives in various places and waved to them. We remarked on the friendliness of the islanders. I returned in time to go on duty at 4:00 pm.

I slept late Sunday morning since church services were scheduled for 10:30 am. At exactly 7:55 am I was awakened by a loud blast. I just knew one of our boilers burst. A second blast followed immediately so I jumped out of bed to see what was happening. At that moment the chief nurse came by and said, "Hurry, get dressed and report to the Quarterdeck, the Japs are bombing us." I dressed in seconds and reported to the officer in charge of the Quarterdeck. Casualties were coming aboard too fast to be treated there, so I was told to report to the operating room. From then on I was assigned permanent duty in the operating room. We were much too busy to worry about the frequent roar of guns, the shaking of the ship and the planes flying overhead. However, reports kept coming to us that the Japanese were using the Solace as a shield while their pilots selected their next target. No one thought about eating but sandwiches and spiked coffee were sent to all wards and the operating room. No one slept that night; the nurses preferred to stay with the patients. During rest periods, the nurses expressed concern about their families on the mainland and how worried they must be rather than concern for themselves.

The next day was a busy one and just as tense as the day before because by this time everyone started to talk and wonder how such a catastrophe could befall Hawaii. Stories of secret codes in local newspapers and caches of ammunition found in various places on the island floated wildly. We even imagined we saw suspicious activity on our hike the Saturday before but we could not be sure. We were told to write short notes to our families to assure them of our safety but all mail was to be censored. Radio contact with the mainland was established but it was several days before we realized how seriously hurt and vulnerable we were. However, not one nurse regretted her assignment to the Solace, rather we considered ourselves as a select group who were proud to serve our country when and where the need was the greatest.

In March of 1942, we sailed for Samoa, then Tonga and later to New Hebrides and New Zealand. On our way to Samoa, we crossed the Equator and thereby became the first group of Navy Nurses to be properly initiated into the mysteries of the deep. We were the first female "shellbacks" and we have official certificates to prove it.

Twenty-seven years later, I retired as a commander in the Nurse Corps and married Cdr. W.W. Willgrube, MSC, USN, Retired. We are living in the small town of Jermyn, Pennsylvania, with only the Lackawanna River to remind us of the sea. Since my husband was at Pearl Harbor during the attack, both of us are life members of the Pearl Harbor Survivors Association.

Harriet Moore Holmes

My recollections of December 7, 1941 begin with being awakened from a sound sleep by night nurses hurriedly returning from a morning stroll in the beautiful gardens located near Tripler General Hospital, informing me that we were being attacked by the Japanese. My first reaction was that this news was someone's idea of a practical joke and I must confess to a feeling of irritation at being awakened in such a manner, as I was not scheduled to report on duty until noon of that Sunday. As I recall, at that time, we were working six days a week with one half of the day free on Sunday.

Within a very few minutes following this sudden awakening, the Chief Nurse's office phoned our quarters with instructions for everyone to report on duty. As we climbed the steps leading from the barracks to the hospital, we could see planes overhead and I recall noting with a sense of horror rising sun insignia on one of the closer ones. Also in the distance, in the direction of Pearl Harbor, black smoke was billowing towards the sky.

As we arrived at the hospital, an unforgettable sight met us. Ambulances were lined up at the entrance, busily carrying in patient after patient. On the exterior porches of the hospital emergency operating tables were being set up and some were already in use for emergency surgery of all types.

Each nurse was assigned to a section of a ward. I recall that the first three patients in each of my assigned beds died within a few minutes and other patients were immediately placed in the beds without even a chance to change the linen. Immediate debridement and intravenous therapy was begun as every patient I saw was severely burned. At this point in reflection, it is interesting to recall how invaluable the training of a nurse can be, for I remember so well that the sense of shock and fear that I at first felt suddenly disappeared and I began functioning with all senses fully alert to the needs of the moment and with no feeling of any personal involvement, an attitude so essential in performing efficiently in a crisis. The day progressed amidst a scene of suffering and death that I have never again witnessed. About 5:00 pm, I was instructed to go to my quarters and attempt to obtain some rest and to report at 7:00 pm for night duty. Needless to say, after the events of the day, it was impossible to sleep, but I did obtain a little rest.

Then came the first night on duty which I shall never forget. No lights of any kind were allowed that would be discernable from the outside. Makeshift blackout arrangements were provided with blankets at the windows of the nurses' offices and kitchens. We were issued flashlights with blue paper covering the light to observe our patients by, making them all appear slightly cyanotic as I recall. Many narcotics had been issued with most of them unrecorded and I recall being asked to attempt to account for as many as possible that each of us had given.

Then began the task of attempting to organize our charts on each patient, most of whom were unidentified at this point. I recall one amusing incident resulting from the havoc. As I was visiting each patient in the early morning dawn, assembling charts with name, rank and serial number, and extent of injury, in one bed lay a long, lanky Kentuckian. When I asked him where he was injured his reply was, "Ma'am, if you had been shot where I was shot, you wouldn't have been hurt at all." And he wasn't kidding.

Among the most vivid memories of that night were the repeated warnings that the Japanese were probably going to return and possibly attempt an occupation of the Island, as it was a well-known fact that our defenses were completely demolished. This feeling gave rise to the uneasiness and nervousness of the many guards on duty around the hospital, and I recall being accompanied by a corpsman to the mess hall for a light supper around 2 am that first night, and being challenged at every turn by an order to halt and state name and reason for passing. I am sure the attack was planned by the Japanese for the dark of the moon, as I have never seen the world so black as those first few nights following December 7 when even a match was considered an act of espionage.

As time passed, we all became more or less acclimated to existing under total blackout conditions and learned to function quite well under such circumstances.

While the memories of that fateful day in our country's history are often recalled, I have always been grateful that I had the privilege of serving my country and fellow countrymen in the capacity of a Registered Nurse. I can think of no more fulfilling or satisfying role for a young woman to equip herself for at that time or at the present time.

Hubertina Schepers Whetsell

I grew up in the small town of Huntingburg, Indiana. After graduating from St. Mary's Hospital School of Nursing, Evansville, Indiana, I wanted to move on. I worked at Michael Reese Hospital in Chicago, Illinois, until I saved enough money to go to California. I worked at Daneron Hospital, Stockton, California, for a time.

I considered taking a Civil Service position in Alaska but after living in California, I decided to enter the Army Nurse Corps. In 1939, you could work in an Army Hospital as a civilian until there was a vacancy in the Army Nurse Corps. I worked at Letterman General Hospital, San Francisco, California, from March 1939 to September 1939, as a civilian. On September 1, 1939, I took my oath of office as 2nd Lt. in the ANC at Letterman. Incidentally, that was the day Germany invaded Poland.

Wanting to travel, I put in my transfer preference, Philippine Island 1st choice, Hawaii 2nd choice. Late in 1940, nurses returning from the Philippines said, "You don't want to go there. It's not what it used to be." So I changed my preference to Hawaii, first choice.

I received my orders for Tripler General Hospital, Hawaii, and sailed on the Hunter Liggett, March 22, 1941. What a beautiful sight to behold five days later when I went up on deck and in front of us was Diamond Head. I realized that I was in Paradise.

Not having enough quarters at Tripler, 8 nurses including myself were housed at Hickam Field. An ambulance and four cars, that four of us had, furnished our transportation. Later more nurses were housed at Hickam. We really enjoyed life. I met several ships to greet nurses that I knew at Letterman enroute to the Philippines. I had many friends who were taken prisoner in the Philippines. How sad we were when we were moved to the barracks at Tripler December 3, 1941.

On December 7, 1941, I was on duty on Ward II, next to the emergency room. Hearing the planes I thought, the Air Corps is really showing themselves this morning. I went out and saw the Rising Sun Insignia on the planes going over the Hospital quite low. I could not believe it or perhaps I did not want to. When the ambulance drove up to the ER and unloaded casualties I knew it was "The Real McCoy". Later that day we were to hear that expression on the PA system quite often.

The tiring and rewarding work began and lasted 4 days. We sent our patients to the field wards and before the wards were emptied we started getting casualties. What horrifying sights. The most severely injured were selected and lined up for surgery. We treated the other patients on the wards using our discretion on what to do for them and giving morphine and spirits as needed.

Sometime in the afternoon we went to Medical Supply to get our gas masks which we kept until we were discharged.

The hospital was blacked out by nightfall. I believe it was about midnight when some of us went to the barracks for some troubled sleep because we fully expected the Japs to come back. They had a rope tied from Ward I to the barracks. Major Baockman, I believe it was, had a blacked-out flashlight and led the way, all of us holding on to the rope.

One event I will never forget, all the amputees were put on Ward 14 and I was in charge of that ward. Young and old, they were a happy lot even though minus a leg or arm. On December 24 they were included in the first group of casualties to return to the mainland. They presented me with a gift of cologne and a gift card which all had signed. I still have the card.

On Friday, March 13, 1942, I met Lt. Erle Whetsell (Whets) who was stationed at Moanalua Gardens with the 193rd Tank Battalion. We dated for one year and on March 18, 1943 we were married at the Upper Post Chapel, Schofield Barracks. Whets was now a Captain. It was truly a military wedding with an arch of sabers to walk through as we left the chapel and then a ride on a tank with MP escorts to our reception at the Officers Club. However I had received permission to wear a wedding gown instead of my uniform. We spent our honeymoon (five days) at Kona Inn on the Big Island.

Things settled down to a routine except for the Battle of Midway which we did not know was taking place.

Before leaving the Islands in November, we had another second honeymoon at Kona. I sailed on the U.S. United States and after a stop at Letterman for my Army discharge I arrived home December 1, 1943. Our son was born January 5, 1944.

Whets returned to the Mainland in July for schooling at Ft. Knox, Kentucky. We had a great time and he returned to Hawaii in November.

I lived with my mother and settled down to being a mother and housewife. The most exciting event until Whets return was the birth of our daughter Barbara, May 25, 1945.

Whets, then a Major, was returning to the Mainland (on the point system) when the war ended August 15, 1945 and received his discharge from the Army.

We traveled some, having visited three countries in South America, the Virgin Islands, Puerto Rico, and Panama. However, our real travel began when we returned to Hawaii on our 25th wedding anniversary, March 1968. We have been back four times and are amazed at the changes each time. We still have dear friends that we met during the war living on Hawaii, Maui, and Oahu.

Our children: Erle II was drafted into the Army on graduating from West Virginia University. Then OCS at Ft. Knox, Kentucky (Yes, the Tank Corp) then to Korea for a year and back to WVU for his Masters degree. He is married and lives in Bridgeport, West Virginia and works for Owen Illinois Glass Company. Barbara also attended WVU then worked for an airline, is now married and lives in Chicago and has one son.

The West Virginia Chapter of PHSA was chartered this year ('73) and I am proud to be a life member. At present I am the only Whitecap in West Virginia. Nursing has come a long way but no work has been as rewarding as taking care of our boys on that Day of Infamy.

Margaret Olsson

As I awakened that Sunday morning to the sound of the bugle and that wonderful band of the 19th Infantry which played every morning in the Quadrangle of the Infantry Barracks, I thought of the fun I was going to have at the picnic that afternoon on the beach of Haleiwa. The sun was shining and it was such a beautiful morning for this young Army nurse who had been up late the night before helping to usher in a 12-pound baby boy.

Just before 8:00 am, I was working in the nursery bathing infants when there was a loud explosion which shook the hospital. The sound was followed by another explosion and then the sound of planes dog-fighting over the hospital. I thought, "Maneuvers on Sunday?" All of a sudden, a Corpsman was running and yelling, "Stay away from the windows and doors, the Japs are bombing Pearl Harbor." I started crying as I tremblingly told the head nurse we were all going to be killed. She said, "If the women in England can take it, you can too, go to the dispensary and get this medicine refilled." On my return, I saw that the hall was filled with wounded from Wheeler Field who were being given injections of morphine for pain and shock. Another nurse was marking the foreheads with a red letter "M," so that the doctor on the ward would know they had been medicated. As I looked out the window, I saw the lawn strewn with litters of patients covered with blood and red soil.

In a state of shock and disbelief, I was sent to the surgical ward where I took care of the critically wounded who died shortly after being admitted. "Such handsome young men, and so young to die," I thought. Tears flowed easily for me, but I kept busy making beds and caring for the wounded that were brought to my ward and died. Ambulatory patients were sent to their units. Those who remained were a real help to the nurses, setting up cots down the center of the ward and wherever a place was available a bed was squeezed in. The windows were covered with tar paper so light would not show through at night.

Around 11:00 am, I received a message that my picnic date was missing in action. He was with the Dawn Patrol based on a beach and while flying that morning encountered a Jap squadron. He shot down several "Migs" before being hit.

At noon we had dinner at the nurses' quarters. The windows were being covered with tar paper and our Japanese cook served us boiled potatoes and partially cook-boiled chicken. It was tasteless. Our Chief Nurse insisted that we eat as it may be our last meal for quite awhile. I worked until 9:00 pm before feeling my way back to the nurses' quarters in the dark, as I had loaned my flashlight to a friend. It seemed a long time getting to the nurses' quarters because of the darkness outdoors. Frightened and with a tension headache, I went to bed. Friends kept checking on me and poking sleeping pills down my mouth. I did not sleep, so the housemother, Lt. M.E. Mellor, took me to her room and poked more pills down. As I was dozing off to sleep the air raid alarm sounded repeatedly. I arose and dressed on the run to the basement, where we all stayed until the all clear blew.

Presently, I am nursing at the Irwin Army Hospital, Ft. Riley, Kansas. The wounded here have had many limbs saved with antibiotics, bone and skin grafts. The patients here are very young men who aged prematurely during the Vietnam crisis. My ward has been converted into a "Detoxification ward," as drugs are the big problem of today.

Since childhood my hobby has been playing the organ which I continue in my hometown, Junction City, Kansas.